IN HER WORDS

IN
HER
WORDS

A POETRY JOURNAL
for and by women

MARYA LAYTH

**ROCKRIDGE
PRESS**

Cover & Interior Designer: Rachel Haeseker
Art Producer: R. R. Hood
Editor: Erin Nelson
Production Editor: Nora Milman

ISBN: Print 978-1-64611-469-6

R0

TO THE COLLECTIVE FEMALE VOICE.
OURS IS A SUN THAT NEVER SETS.

POETRY IN THE HANDS OF WOMEN IS POWER.

And for this reason, it was long confined to the bedroom or siphoned underground. But then there was Dickinson. Angelou. Lorde. Rich. These voices (and so many more)—uninterested in the status quo or caging their experiences in the private sphere—broke through. By the 1970s, poetry emerged as an explosive tool to release, unite, and resist. Women writing candidly about the personal, the political, and the intersection of identity became a liberating force—both inside and out.

Today's cannon of poetry builds upon the voices of the past. Again, we turn to poetry as incantation—to seek acknowledgment, representation, and demand change. To hold truth to power and navigate the self.

But why this medium?

In Sanskrit, one of the world's oldest and most beautiful languages, the word for "poetry" is *kavi*. Its root *ku* means to cry out. For women, this cry is raw, guttural, essential to our being—evoking a sense of familiarity, universalism, and uniqueness. A lyrical and intuitive expression of deep knowing, it moves us all forward. The examples span across time and place.

Women like Edhenuanna, the first known poet and High Priestess of the most important temple in Sumer, Mesopotamia, used poetry to bring stability to the empire. Her hymns united the rivaling divinities and created a bridge between people of opposing beliefs. Juana Inés de la Cruz, the no-nonsense nun of 17th-century Spanish-occupied Mexico, wrote impassioned poems to her female partner to validate her love long before the term "lesbian" existed in the Latin dialect.

Sarojini Naidu, a revered Indian poet who lived under patriarchal colonial rule, became the first female governor of an Indian state. Her words were instrumental in achieving India's independence. And these are just three women whose poetry has lit the darkest places of human history.

Yet even when we feel empowered by the remarkable poets before and beside us, it can be daunting to put our own pen to the page. That's why I read, watched, and listened to hours of interviews and public statements by hundreds of female-identifying poets, hoping their insights might inspire your own self-expression. I will let their words guide you, only asking that as you pour yourself into this journal, you do not ever apologize for the way you take up space on the page. For how many times you need to cross out the same verse. For the days, weeks, or months you take leave from writing.

I believe creativity is there to serve you. If you choose to write in iambic meter, great. If you prefer free verse, wonderful. If you want to reinvent form itself, lovely. If you want to read at an open mic, power to you. If you only ever recite these poems to your cat, that's brilliant too. Poetry should never be one more thing you feel pressured to conform to.

The poets featured in *In Her Words*—women of all ages, races, time periods, sexual orientations, gender identities, and cultures—are united by the desire to be close to their truths. It is the commitment to be close to ours that connects us to their legacies.

> *"... my investment in justice and liberation and my interest in literature could not be separated."*
>
> JOSHUA JENNIFER ESPINOZA

*"I have to show the world
I'm here and why I'm here."*

ELIZABETH ACEVEDO

> *"What are the tyrannies you swallow day by day and attempt to make your own . . . in silence?"*
>
> AUDRE LORDE

> *"Learn from tradition,*
> *but don't be afraid to break it."*
>
> MONG-LAN

"*I always feel better for having pinned the beast down—but whole weeks have been ruined by keeping it in my throat.*"

MEGAN FALLEY

> *"I think there are three pillars of storytelling: bravery, authenticity, and vulnerability—and my promise to myself is to live in those three pillars."*
>
> CLEO WADE

> "... there's a presence inside of words.
> The Ojibwe say that each word has a spirit."
>
> LOUISE ERDRICH

> *"Writing, like many other things in life,*
> *is often an act of trembling faith."*
> ĐỖ NGUYÊN MAI

> *"To be both woman and poet is to be Goddess of creation, it's to be mother of some sort even when we are not trying to be."*
>
> MERCEDEZ HOLTRY

"The world really needs you to find what you want to do and do it."

JESSICA SEMAAN

> *"Just as I believe that the scientist is exploring the frontiers of boundaries . . . of the physical world . . . I am convinced that the artist and poet is out on the frontiers of human consciousness . . . continually asking why."*
>
> CLARIBEL ALEGRÍA

> *"To express something well is not a question of having a top-class education and understanding poetic forms: rather, it's a question of paying attention."*
> ALICE OSWALD

"There is a level of surprise always involved. You cannot say it's going to turn out like this, or it's going to turn out like that ... Poetry could go any way."

NUALA NÍ DHOMHNAILL

> *"Trust your instincts and allow yourself the patience and time to discover your voice."*
>
> ARIANA BROWN

_____

_____

_____

_____

_____

_____

_____

_____

_____

_____

_____

_____

_____

_____

_____

_____

"IMAGINATION ALLOWS US TO FEEL AND EXPRESS THOSE THINGS THAT MIGHT DESTROY US IN ANY OTHER FORM."

NTOZAKE SHANGE

> *"I write poems to figure things out.
> I think of 'poem' as a verb, as in: to
> poem my way through something."*
>
> SARAH KAY

"I don't care about stigma, shame, or bravado. Writing is cathartic for me, a lifeline. It's about survival and mental health as much as it is about creativity and expression."

WARSAN SHIRE

"Women are about making strength out of powerlessness."

FATEMA MERNISSI

"I am seeking the body on the page, even the broken body, even the ecstatic body— even the broken and ecstatic body. I am looking for a field for the body to run in."

NATALIE DIAZ

"*PEOPLE GREATLY INSPIRE ME: THEIR WORLD, STORIES, FRUSTRATIONS, CONFUSION, SADNESS, HAPPINESS, PAIN, PASSION.*"

NUJOOM ALGHANEM

> *"... because at its heart,*
> *real writing is listening to yourself."*
> MOOKIE KATIGBAK-LACUESTA

> *"... you're always fighting to find out what it is you want to say. You have to go deeper and deeper each time."*
>
> ANNE SEXTON

> *"Across cultures, poets have traditionally been the seekers, the seers, the diviners— seeing things other people couldn't."*
> TISHANI DOSHI

"It is a labor of love to harness your voice into existence when the spaces you inhabit are not expecting to hear your story."

KARLA CORDERO

....

....

....

....

....

....

....

....

....

....

....

....

....

....

....

....

....

....

....

"Beware; for I am fearless, and therefore powerful."

MARY SHELLEY

> *"The writer's life is a constant battle to balance your responsibility to your writing with your responsibilities to the everyday world . . . there's that constant pull of the world, which is opposed to the need to clear out a kind of psychic space with plenty of time and no interruptions."*
>
> LESLIE MARMON SILKO

"Women are writing not only because writing is emancipatory, powerful, radical, revolutionary—but also because I personally believe that political spaces . . . often tend to impede rather than facilitate women's participation."

MEENA KANDASAMY

....

....

....

....

....

....

....

....

....

....

....

....

....

....

....

> *"To me women's lib means a fuller development of her personality, so that, she does not have to ask for freedom. She herself develops a capacity to achieve it."*
>
> AMRITA PRITAM

"If we're not in the real world, how are we going to be in touch with our stories?"
RUPI KAUR

"I've always been fascinated by—or perhaps haunted by—the limits of language. With poetry you get to investigate all of the weird things you can make words do."

MELISSA LOZADA-OLIVA

*"... poetry is the only creative writing art form
that builds breath into it. It makes you breathe.
It not only allows for silence, it demands it.
We enter the poem with our own breath."*

ADA LIMÓN

> *"Poetry is this space of play where you can figure out who you are."*
>
> TRACE PETERSON

*"I still believe that poetry is not medicine—
it's an X-ray. It helps you see the wound and
understand it. We all feel alienated because of
this continuous violence in the world . . . so we
resort to poetry as a possibility for survival."*
DUNYA MIKHAIL

"Certainly there's no time to be boring..."
FRANNY CHOI

"VERY RARELY DO YOU HEAR ANYONE SAY THEY WRITE THINGS DOWN AND FEEL WORSE. IT'S AN ACT THAT HELPS YOU, PRESERVES YOU, ENERGIZES YOU IN THE VERY DOING OF IT."

NAOMI SHIHAB NYE

> *"The only connection I know to exist between woman and poet is inside of my body and the bodies of those who identify the same."*
>
> SAROYA MARSH

*"Poetry is a political act because
it involves telling the truth."*

JUNE JORDAN

"Poetry asks us to be as honest as possible. To say the thing that has been boiling inside of us . . . . It's the way we talk back to the thing that has hurt us."

DENICE FROHMAN

> *"... it's the strange and wonderful thing about writing poetry—you can never predict where or when or even why something moves you to write a poem."*
>
> ELIZABETH BISHOP

"SOMETIMES I AM AFRAID BUT MY SPIRIT SAYS WRITE IT. I HAVE TO RISE UP IN THAT MOMENT AND WRITE."

NAYYIRAH WAHEED

> *"Creativity cannot be regulated nor should it be. Who would know this better than a woman writer..."*
>
> KISHWAR NAHEED

> *"Words are vehicles for bringing something into being: a vision of peace, a vision of connection, a vision of telling a story of who we are, what we've done, where we've been, where we're going."*
>
> JOY HARJO

"If a poem can make somebody feel somewhat less isolated . . . then the poem's done its job."

YRSA DALEY-WARD

"As women we are always shifting and taking on new shapes . . . I stand tall in that truth."

ALEXANDRA ELLE

"... when you write a poem, you write it for anybody and everybody ... it's a gift to yourself but it's a gift to anybody who has a hunger for it."

MARY OLIVER

"Poems can become public acts of bravery but the actual writing of them often feels like private cowardice. Shutting the world out or up to be left alone with thoughts and feelings, so as to be able to make announcements to the tub and shower curtain . . ."

AMANDA NADELBERG

*"I'm not sure what the function of poetry is . . .
but I know we're in trouble when we start
talking about what poetry 'ought' to do."*

MARGARET ATWOOD

"Poetry is breathing. The world and universe are going on all around us all the time. Being a poet is holding in the inhalations, the music of the world, the beautiful and the horrendous..."

ALLISON ADELLE HEDGE COKE

> *"We can't deny one body and favor another body. As far as my spiritual level of experience is concerned, the woman is the core part of humanity."*
>
> HUDA SHARAWI

"Poetry, like all literature . . . helps change culture because it changes individuals."

DAWN LUNDY MARTIN

> *"Poetry has absolutely made it possible for me to figure out how I want to be alive."*
>
> TC TOLBERT

> *"I only intend to write what insists on being written, and what I need to write in order to evolve."*
>
> LADAN OSMAN

> *"I celebrate the lives of women, our work,*
> *the relationships we have with others,*
> *and the one we have with ourselves."*
>
> LANG LEAV

"Your voice is wild and simple. You are untranslatable into any one tongue."
ANNA AKHMATOVA

"BEING AN ARTIST IS THE PROCESS OF CREATING, NOT WHAT COMES FROM IT AT THE END."

ANDREA GIBSON

REVISITING YOUR WORK

For just a moment, think of this journal as a forest and the poems you have written as a trail through the wild. Choose three of your pieces and reflect on the following for each.

Is the trail clear?
Are there any parts of the poem you find yourself tripping over? Reading your poem out loud can be helpful toward this end. Go a step further by recording yourself, playing it back, and listening to each poem as objectively as possible.

Do the views along the trail make for an interesting walk?
Are you using vivid imagery, or are there other ways to express yourself more creatively? Some of the most powerful writing abides by this basic rule: *show don't tell*. Describing the view is more impactful than merely stating it is beautiful.

Did the trail lead where the map said it would?
What is your intention with the poem and did you achieve it? Some poems are barefaced confessions; some help us find our way back to our own truth. Others are a blatant call for change. All are valid. Just remain mindful of being deliberate.

As you go through this exercise, remember there is no shame in revision. Explore each poem knowing there is no right or wrong amount of time you can spend on it. You might find yourself wrestling with a poem for months before it feels right, or it can be instantaneous. The length of editing time is inconsequential—what matters is that you feel authentic in your expression.

WHERE TO SUBMIT YOUR WORK

If you are interested in publishing your poetry, consider submitting to a literary journal. As a starting point, you can adhere to the list below.

Be sure to carefully read each journal's mission statement. Even if you submit your most profound narrative resistance poem, a journal that only publishes haikus about aliens will likely not feature your revolutionary masterpiece.

Remember that while publication can be validating, poetry is about practice. It's in that solitary space where poetry has intrinsic value. If there's one thing I hope you've taken away from the women's quotes in this—your—journal, it's to not let anything come between you and your love of writing.

The Acentos Review

The Acentos Review publishes poetry by the international community of Latinx writers at various stages of their careers and accepts submissions in English, Spanish, Portuguese, a combination of two languages, and indigenous languages. Accepts submissions on a rolling basis.

@acentosreview
acentosreview.com

The Adroit Journal

The Adroit Journal showcases bold, experimental, and inventive poetry by young and emerging writers from around the world. New issues are published multiple times a year. Check the website for updated reading periods.

@adroitjournal
theadroitjournal.org

African American Review

African American Review features insightful poetry by and for the African American community and has featured prominent writers such as Toni Morrison and Rita Dove. New issues are published every spring, summer, fall, and winter. Accepts submissions between September 15 and May 15.

aar.slu.edu

Atlanta Review

Atlanta Review is an international, award-winning publication known for its reputation of blind-reading and publishing poetry based on craftsmanship. New issues are published biannually. Accepts submissions throughout the year with the exception of December and June.

@ATLReview

atlantareview.com

Black Warrior Review

Black Warrior Review is the oldest literary journal run by graduate students in the United States. It publishes both emerging and established writers. Accepts submissions between December 1 and March 1 and June 1 and September 1.

@BlackWarriorRev

bwr.ua.edu

Boulevard Magazine

Boulevard Magazine looks for innovative work by previously published and unpublished writers. Accepts submissions between October 1 and May 1.

@BoulevardLitMag

boulevardmagazine.org

Cordella Magazine

Cordella Magazine represents unique narratives by women and non-binary people and is especially looking for work about spiritual life, ecology, and community. New issues are published annually. Accepts submissions between July 1 and September 6.

@cordellamag
cordella.org

Crab Fat Magazine

Crab Fat Magazine encourages submissions by those "flattened in the media," including all POC, queer/trans, disabled, femme, nonbinary, neurodivergent, trauma survivors, and nonreligious persons. Accepts submissions on a rolling basis.

@CrabFatMagazine
crabfatmagazine.com

Deaf Poets Society

Deaf Poets Society seeks to provide a platform for the deaf and/or disabled community and is especially interested in featuring poetry about illness from the perspectives of all identities. Accepts submissions on a rolling basis.

@thedeafpoets
deafpoetssociety.com

Dying Dahlia Review

Dying Dahlia Review publishes female-identifying writers with an emphasis on poetry that is brief and powerful. Accepts submissions on a rolling basis.

@DyingDahliaRev
dyingdahliareview.com

Gertrude Press

Gertrude Press is proudly distinguished as the longest-running queer journal. Accepts submissions on a rolling basis.

@gertrudepress

gertrudepress.org

Hyphen Magazine

Hyphen Magazine is particularly interested in emerging artists who write about issues affecting Asian Americans in an original, inventive, and accurate manner. New poetry is published monthly. Accepts submissions on a rolling basis.

@hyphenmag

hyphenmagazine.com

Jaggery

Jaggery is a publication for and by poets of the South-Asian diaspora and also welcomes those who experience a meaningful connection with South Asians. New issues are published multiple times a year. Check the website for updated reading periods.

@JaggeryLitMag

jaggerylit.com

Kenyon Review

Kenyon Review is a multiplatform publication known worldwide for publishing the best in contemporary poetry. The literature journal features writers at various stages of their careers—from Nobel Laureates to the most daring new voices. New issues are published five times a year. Check the website for updated reading periods.

@kenyonreview

kenyonreview.org

Kweli Journal

Kweli Journal publishes poetry by emerging writers of color and seeks to give these narratives a platform to impact communities around the world. New issues are published triannually. Accepts submissions between September 1 and May 30.

> *@kwelijournal*
> *kwelijournal.org*

Lavender Review

Lavender Review is an international e-zine appealing to a lesbian readership and is looking for poetry by, about, and for lesbians. New issues are published biannually. Check the website for updated reading periods.

> *lavrev.net*

Meridians

Meridians is an intersectional feminist journal that publishes poetry by and about women of color in various global contexts. Accepts submissions on a rolling basis.

> *sophia.smith.edu/meridians*

Minola Review

Minola Review publishes work by female-identifying and nonbinary poets who are unafraid of exploring the uncomfortable. New poetry is published on a monthly basis.

> *@ReviewMinola*
> *minolareview.com*

Mizna

Mizna represents the narratives of Arab and Muslim poets and artists. It is currently the only Arab American literary magazine in the United States. New issues are published annually. Check the website for updated reading periods.

@Mizna_ArabArt
mizna.org

Plenitude Magazine

Plenitude Magazine features exceptional poetry about queer histories, cultures, experiences, and sensibilities, but is particularly interested in submissions by LGBTQ2S+-identifying persons. Accepts submissions on a rolling basis.

@PlenitudeMag
plenitudemagazine.ca

Pretty Owl Poetry

Pretty Owl Poetry is a feminist journal particularly interested in showcasing work about the bodily experience of women, nonbinary, and trans people. New issues are published four times a year. Check the website for updated reading periods.

@PrettyOwlPoetry
prettyowlpoetry.com

Raspa Magazine

Raspa Magazine gives greater visibility to queer Latinx poets and encourages submissions from anyone who identifies as LGBTQ+. Accepts submissions between February 15 and August 15.

@RaspaMagazine
raspamagazine.com

Rattle

Rattle exists to remind the public that language can be as moving as mainstream entertainment. It publishes poets whose work achieves this end. Accepts submissions on a rolling basis.

@RattleMag

rattle.com

THRUSH Poetry Journal

THRUSH Poetry Journal accepts a diverse array of poetry and nominates featured pieces for most major prizes, anthologies, and awards.

@thrushjournal

thrushpoetryjournal.com

Transition Magazine

Transition Magazine, a publication of the Hutchins Center for African & African American Research at Harvard University, is a literary journal that publishes poetry reflecting on race as it relates to Africa and the diaspora. Accepts submissions on a rolling basis.

@Transition_Mag

hutchinscenter.fas.harvard.edu/transition

RESOURCES

A Change of World: Poetry and the Women's Movement

An insightful podcast on the history of poetry as it relates to the women's movement.

wnyc.org/story/change-world-poetry-and-womens-movement/

All Poetry

An alternative to in-person writing groups. *All Poetry* is an online poetry community where participants submit and critique each other's work.

allpoetry.com

Button Poetry

The official YouTube channel by the publication *Button Poetry* providing daily spoken word performances by the leading voices in contemporary poetry.

youtube.com/user/ButtonPoetry

Duotrope

The most comprehensive search engine for writers of all genres looking for literary journals and publishers.

duotrope.com

Poets & Writers

One of the leading online and print nonprofit literary organizations in the United States. Their website and bimonthly print magazine feature an updated list of conferences, workshops, contests, and reading periods for publications worldwide.

pw.org

Poetry Barn

A website featuring online writing workshops.

poetrybarn.co/about

SlamFind

An application to stay current with the North American slam-poetry scene. *SlamFind* is a platform that allows its users to watch poetry videos, stream live poetry performances, and find local, regional, and national poetry events.

slamfind.vhx.tv

ABOUT THE AUTHOR

Marya Layth is a poet, recreational fantasy writer—whatever that means—and a visual artist. Sometimes she likes to say her poetry out loud in a room full of strangers. Sometimes she likes to create art for her poetry that she shares on the internet. Sometimes she likes to send it to literary journals and see what happens.

Once, *Write Bloody Publishing* chose her working poetry collection as a finalist. More than once, she has been featured in some pretty neat literary journals. One of those literary journals nominated her poem from said collection for Best of the Net. That was a warm feeling.

You can also purchase her original poetry and art on Redbubble: www.redbubble.com/people/maryalayth. When she isn't doing any of the above, she is probably looking for a home for her working poetry collection while she keeps it real with her cat somewhere in New Jersey. You can find her on Instagram @marya.layth, Twitter @maryalayth, and Facebook @laythmarya.